EARTHQUAKES

Ellen J. Prager

illustrated by **Susan Greenstein**

NATIONAL GEOGRAPHIC
WASHINGTON, D.C.

To all those who have dedicated their lives to earthquake research, education, preparation, and rescue in the aftermath of disaster. –EJP

For my wonderful family, Phil, my husband, and Gina, my daughter, who both help me to see what is special about each day. –SG

SHAKE, RATTLE, AND ROLL…
Buildings, trees, and the ground sway when the Earth gives way.

EARTHQUAKE!

Earthquakes happen on Earth every day. Most are small—too small to feel. But at least once a week, there is a strong earthquake somewhere on the planet.

A strong earthquake can mean disaster for people who live nearby. The ground shakes, jumps, and rolls while people run for safety. Buildings may crack or crumble. Roads can be ripped apart.

What causes an earthquake?

Earthquakes happen when rocks inside the land or under the sea break apart. Rocks can break when they are squeezed, stretched, or pulled in different directions.

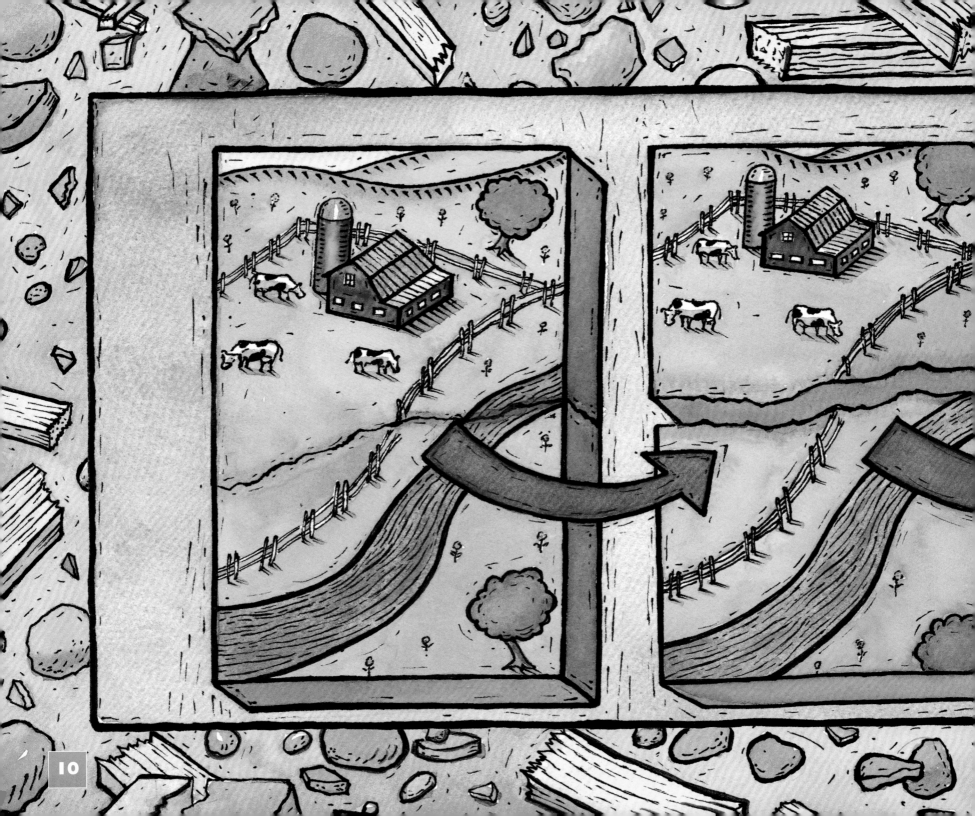

Rocks break sort of like
a rubber band that has been
stretched too far. If the rocks are
stretched, squeezed, or pulled too
much, they split apart—then snap
back slightly out of place.

When rocks break, lots of energy is
released. Where does the energy go?

Breaking rocks send energy into the ground. The energy causes the ground to move in what we call an earthquake. To a person, an earthquake can feel like shaking, a sudden jolt, or a slow roll. An earthquake can last for just a few short seconds or go on for several very long minutes.

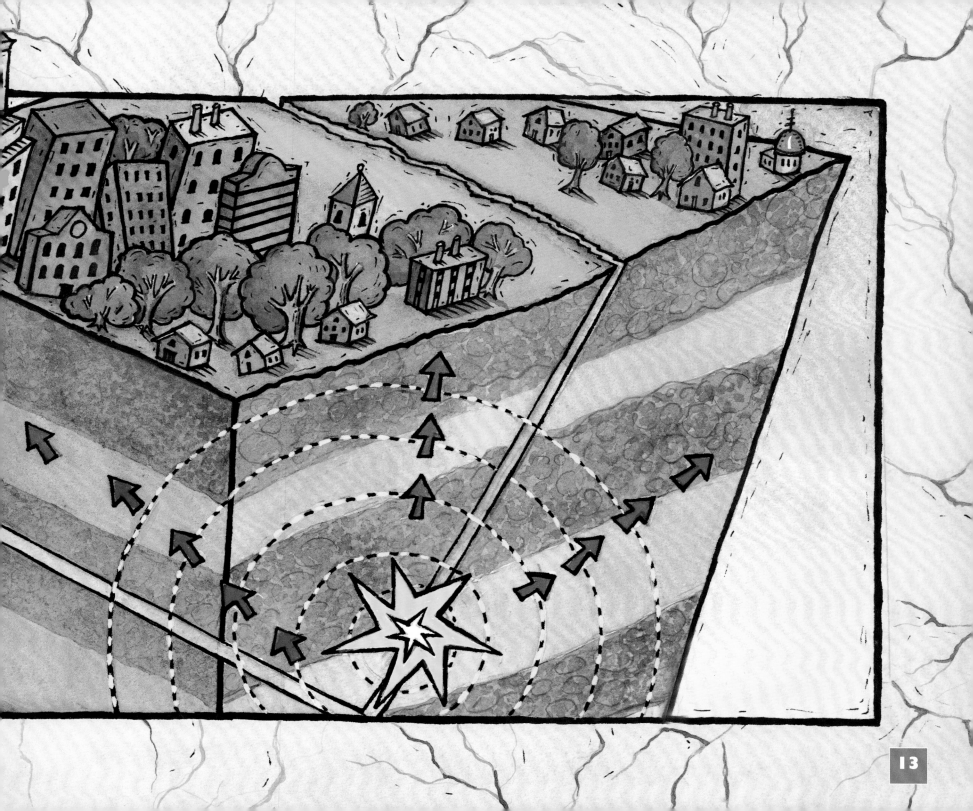

Most earthquakes happen because Earth's outer surface is moving. Like a huge jigsaw puzzle, the planet's outer surface is made up of big pieces called plates. These plates move very slowly in different directions, so slowly you can't feel them moving. Over time, the plates slide, slip, and bump into each other along their edges.

Pacific Plate

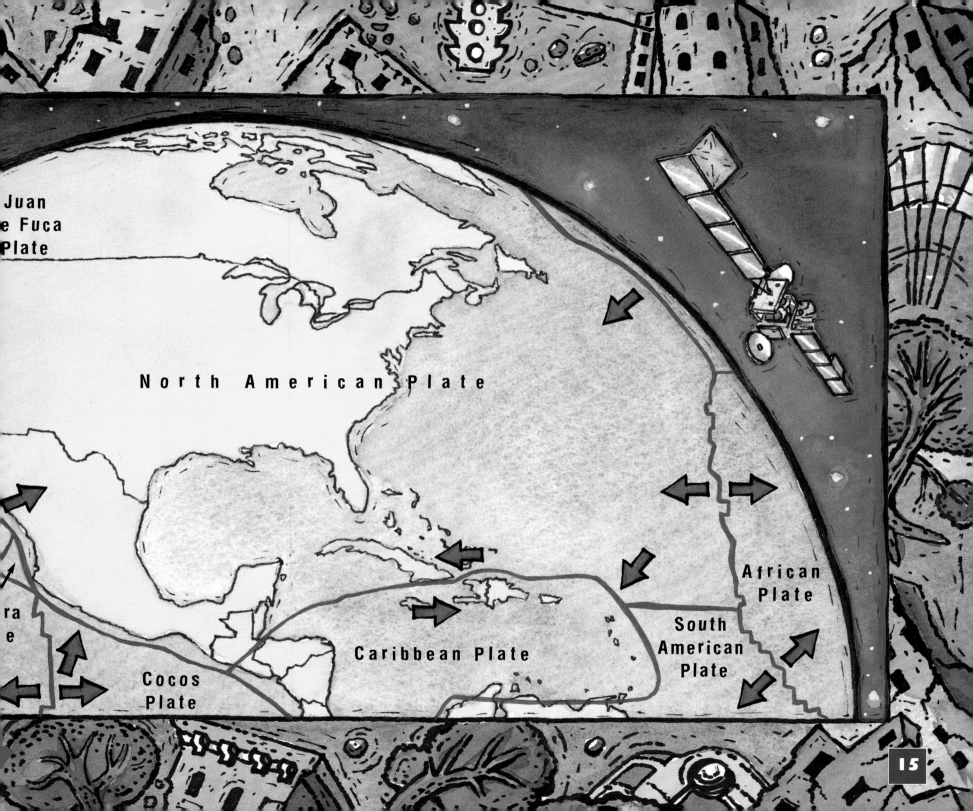

Most earthquakes happen along the edges of Earth's big plates.

Look at the map showing earthquake activity. Can you name two places where earthquakes happen most often?

EARTHQUAKES

Pacific Ocean

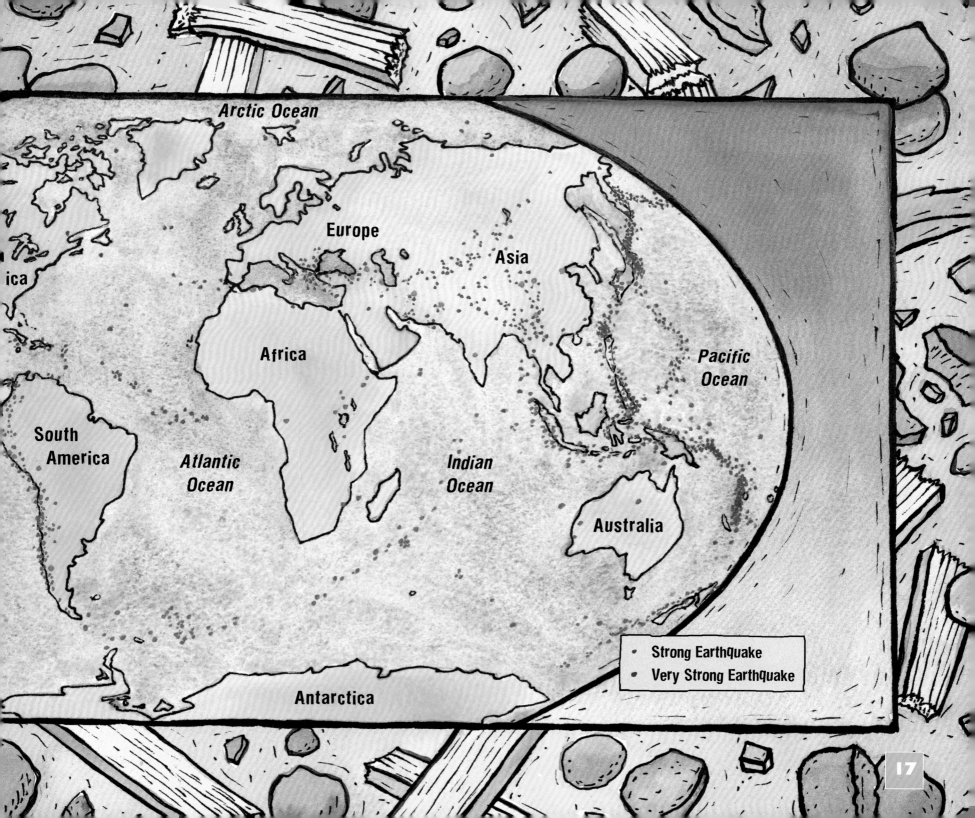

San Andreas Fault
CLOSE-UP VIEW

Earthquakes are common in California, especially along the famous San Andreas Fault. Two of Earth's big plates meet at the San Andreas Fault. These two plates move in different directions. Over time, the rocky edges of the two plates bump and stick together, slowly stretching and pulling. Every once in a while, the rocky edges break, release energy, and cause earthquakes.

San Francisco

CALIFORNIA

Los Angeles

Pacific
Ocean

San Andreas Fault

In an earthquake, the ground may move up, down, or sideways. Sideways motion is very dangerous because it can cause tall buildings to sway back and forth or weak houses to collapse. In areas where earthquakes are common, people are learning how to build homes and buildings that will stay safe when the ground moves.

In places where the ground is made of soft sand, shaking can cause buildings to sink down and tumble over. Where earthquakes happen, buildings and homes should be specially designed and be built on solid ground.

FORESHOCK

24

Sometimes there are many small earthquakes before the big one. These are called foreshocks. After the big earthquake—the mainshock—again there may be many small quakes. These are called aftershocks.

MAINSHOCK

AFTERSHOCK

EARTHQUAKE SAFETY

1. Stay calm during an earthquake.

2. If outside, find an open space away from power poles, buildings, fences, etc.

3. If inside, stay away from windows. Take cover under a sturdy desk, table, or door frame.

4. Listen for instructions from a teacher or parent, or listen to the radio for information.

No one has found a sure way to predict earthquakes, so the best protection is to be prepared and know what to do. Find a safe place and stay away from things that could come crashing down.

We cannot prevent
earthquakes from
happening. Earthquakes
are part of Earth's
changing nature.

Scientists study earthquakes to learn more about them and to help prevent injury and damage. One day we may be able to predict earthquakes and give people more warning.

Have you ever felt an earthquake?

Create your own earthquake

Here's what you'll need:

- **A square or rectangular baking pan**
- **Enough sand to fill the pan about halfway**
- **A brick or a fist-size flat rock**

1. Place the sand in the baking pan and pack it down so that the surface is smooth and flat.

2. Place the brick or rock on the sand. Does it stay on top of the sand or sink?

3. Now shake the pan back and forth.

What happens?

The brick or rock now sinks into the sand or falls over!

What did you discover? (use a mirror to read)

You were the earthquake. If the brick or rock had been a house built on loose sand, the house would have sunk into the ground. Walls might have cracked, and rooms might have collapsed. In places where earthquakes are likely to happen, buildings should be built on solid ground and follow strict safety codes.

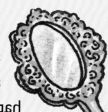

To create her paintings, Susan Greenstein used black ink and watercolor paint on watercolor paper.

Reprinted in paperback and library binding, 2017
Paperback ISBN: 978-1-4263-2833-6
Reinforced library binding ISBN: 978-1-4263-2834-3

Book design by LeSales Dunworth
Text is set in Gill Sans. Display text is set in Dirtyhouse, and some is hand-lettered.

Jump Into Science series consultant: Gary Brockman, Early Education Science Specialist

Earthquake safety tips adapted from *National Geographic World* article: "With a Jolt: Earthquakes Shatter Houses—and Lives," by David George Gordon, January 1998.

The Library of Congress cataloged the 2002 edition as follows:
Prager, Ellen J.
Earthquakes / by Ellen J. Prager ; illustrated by Susan Greenstein.
p. cm. — (Jump into science)
ISBN 0-7922-8202-7
1. Earthquakes—Juvenile literature. [1. Earthquakes.] I. Greenstein, Susan, ill. II. Title. III. Series.
QE521.3 .P727 2002
551.22—dc21
2001000686

Since 1888, the National Geographic Society has funded more than 12,000 research, exploration, and preservation projects around the world. The Society receives funds from National Geographic Partners, LLC, funded in part by your purchase. A portion of the proceeds from this book supports this vital work. To learn more, visit natgeo.com/info.

For more information, visit nationalgeographic.com, call 1-800-647-5463, or write to the following address:
National Geographic Partners, LLC
1145 17th Street N.W.
Washington, D.C. 20036-4688 U.S.A.

National Geographic supports K-12 educators with ELA Common Core Resources. Visit natgeoed.org/commoncore for more information.

Printed in China
17/RRDS/1

DR. ELLEN J. PRAGER writes on geology and marine-related topics for children and adults. She's the author of two other Jump Into Science books—*Sand* (A *Parents' Choice* winner for 2001) and *Volcano!* She lives in Arlington, Virginia.

SUSAN GREENSTEIN has illustrated numerous children's books and magazine articles. Her work has also appeared in exhibits from New York to Los Angeles. She earned a B.F.A. from Pratt Institute and an M.S.E. from Queens College. She lives in Brooklyn, New York.

EDUCATIONAL EXTENSIONS

1. What kind of damage can you expect from an earthquake that has sideways motion and happens in a place with ground made of soft sand?

2. Are earthquakes common in Japan? Why or why not?

3. What does "energy" have to do with earthquakes?